The Four Magic Questions of Screenwriting:

Structure Your Screenplay Fast

By Marilyn Horowitz

ISBN: 978-0-9799089-0-3

Library of Congress Cataloging Number

Other books by Marilyn Horowitz:

How to Write a Screenplay in Ten Weeks Using the Horowitz System®
Copyright © 2007 by Marilyn Horowitz

How to Write a Screenplay Using the Horowitz System® – *The High School Edition*
Copyright © 2008 by Marilyn Horowitz

How to Write a Screenplay Using the Horowitz System® – *The Middle School Edition*
Copyright © 2008 by Marilyn Horowitz

How to Write a Screenplay Using the Horowitz System® – *The Middle School Edition: Film Breakdowns Supplement*
Copyright © 2009 by Marilyn Horowitz

Table of Contents

The Four Magic Questions of Screenwriting – Breakdown of Witness

Introduction   1

Chapter 1: What Are The Four Magic Questions of Screenwriting?   5

Chapter 2: How The Four Magic Questions of Screenwriting Work   19

Chapter 3: Question 1 (Act I): *What is the Main Character's Dream?*   33

Chapter 4: Question 2 (Act II, Part 1): *What is the Main Character's Worst Nightmare?*   41

Chapter 5: Question 3 (Act II, Part 2): *Who or What Would They "Die" for?*   49

Chapter 6: Question 4 (Act III): *What is the Resolution of the Dream or a New Dream?*   57

Emergency BONUS Chapter How to Find or Refine Your Screenplay Idea   67

Chapter 7: Putting It All Together   85

Appendix   99

Suggested Films   101

Acknowledgements   102

Publishing Information   103

The Four Magic Questions of Screenwriting –

ACT I	ACT II, Part 1
Magic Question 1	**Magic Question 2**
What is the main character's dream?	What is the main character's worst nightmare?

Sequence 1.

An Amish funeral is held for Rachel Lapp's husband, Jacob (3:41)

Daniel, who yearns for Rachel, consoles the grieving widow (5:30)

Samuel and Rachel go to the city, Daniel and Rachel's uncle, Eli, see them off (7:53)

Train to Baltimore is delayed, Samuel and Rachel must wait in the station (10:20)

Sequence 2.

While in the station bathroom, Samuel witnesses a murder (13:46)

McFee hears Samuel and searches stalls, but does not catch him (15:44)

Detective John Book interviews Samuel about the murder (17:14)

Sequence 3.

Rachel does not want any part of the investigation (20:44)

John makes her stay the night at his sister Elaine's house (21:28)

Rachel reiterates her wish to leave (23:03)

Samuel recognizes McFee in a newspaper clipping at the police department (27:54)

Sequence 4.

John goes to see Chief Schaeffer to tell him about McFee (29:40)

John doesn't trust people in the department and wants Samuel and Rachel moved (30:41)

McFee tries to kill John, only wounds him (31:34)

John calls his partner, Elden Carter, and tells him to get rid of all files on the Lapps (33:40)

Sequence 5.

John returns Samuel and Rachel to their Amish town (36:25)

Weakened, John crashes his car (37:08)

Rachel wants her fellow villagers to treat John's wound (39:45)

Rachel takes care of feverish John (42:00)

Chief Schaeffer and McFee try to find Rachel (44:37)

Sequence 6.

Samuel finds John's gun. Rachel disapproves (46:25)

Eli tells Samuel about guns, wars and killing (49:18)

With Eli, John visits local general store to call Carter (54:38)

Samuel shows John various things around the farm (56:50)

Eli tells John to help him milk the cows (57:51)

John meets Daniel (60:30)

Since many films are two hours long, especially classic films, the basis for the 12 sequences is a hypothetical 120-minute film. By looking at films in 10-minute sequences, it's easier to understand them. Note that one page of screenplay in proper format equals approximately one minute of screen time. Try for between 90 and 120 pages total.

Breakdown of *Witness*

ACT II, Part 2	ACT III
Magic Question 3	**Magic Question 4**
Who or what would they "die" for?	What is the resolution of the dream or a new dream?

Sequence 7.

John fixes his car battery, is able to get the radio working (64:47)

John and Rachel dance (66:00)

Eli catches them and reprimands Rachel (67:13)

Rachel asserts herself to Eli (68:46)

Chief Schaeffer questions Carter about John's whereabouts (69:00)

Sequence 8.

John helps raise a barn. Daniel mentions him leaving in passing (71:20)

Rumors are being spread about John and Rachel (77:08)

John sees Rachel partially naked, but does not approach her (79:45)

John tells Rachel that they live in separate worlds, and one of them must cross over in order for them to be together. He decides not to (81:05)

Sequence 9.

John learns that Carter has been killed (82:40)

John calls Chief Schaeffer and threatens him (84:00)

John assaults a man who is taunting the Amish (85:56)

John and Rachel kiss–a goodbye to what could have been (90:15)

Sequence 10.

Chief Schaeffer finds out where the Amish town is (93:00)

McFee and his partner hunt John (95:20)

John kills Fergie, McFee's co-conspirator, and takes his gun (102:00)

John shoots McFee (102:26)

Sequence 11.

Chief Schaeffer takes Rachel hostage (103:00)

John convinces Chief Schaeffer not to shoot him, disarms him (104:36)

Sequence 12.

Police arrive to wrap up investigation (105:07)

John says goodbye to Samuel (106:26)

John goes to see Rachel and he can't say goodbye to her (107:45)

John waves goodbye to Eli (108:25)

Driving out of the village, he says goodbye to Daniel (109:01)

Introduction

My job is to teach people how to write good scripts. Everyone has an idea for an interesting screenplay, because movies are about what happens in people's lives and how we respond to the challenges life presents. Haven't we all had a wonderful or terrifying life event and come away thinking that the story would make a great movie? We all have similar experiences, but each of us processes things in a unique way. If you think you have a good idea, I can help you to find your story by using The Four Magic Questions of Screenwriting.

How The Four Magic Questions of Screenwriting Will Benefit You

- Organize your screenplay quickly and with confidence

- Write a better, more original story with surprising plot twists and turns

- Create complex, living characters with clear wants and needs

- Have fun, because you know what you're doing

- Write good dialogue, because you know what your characters would say

- Rewrite easily by giving you a fresh perspective

The Right Way or the Long Way?

I believe that making up stories should be fun. I have found that there's a right way and a long way to write a screenplay, and this is the right way. Other methods push you to create plot first and then fit your characters into that story. This is backwards thinking. After more than 10 years of teaching screenwriting, it's clear to me that the way writing is often taught makes the process harder than it has to be. If you try to force your characters into a plot too early in the creation process, the script will feel contrived and be hard to rewrite. The rewriting process is critical to the successful creation of a screenplay, because all good writing is the result of rewriting. To summarize, using this book will allow you to develop characters quickly and deeply, and to organize and structure a better plot with ease.

How to Use This Book

The book is interactive. Just read and respond to the questions as they are asked. Fill in boxes where prompted. Use a pencil so you can relax and write your first thoughts. Complete the exercises to find the answer to the questions asked. In several of the exercises, you'll be asked to use a timer. Please try it and see if it works for you. As you read, ask yourself, "What would I have done if I were the main character in my own script? What would I not have done? What then, would my character do or not do?" If you know what you would have done, you can figure out how your character would have behaved. Take chances and challenge your imagination. You can always fix problems later. To show you how this works, I'll be using examples from several successful films, and will be using the film *Witness* as the central example. A breakdown of the film appears in the beginning of this book, and is a simple, visual way of describing the sequence of events that answer each of The Four Magic Questions of Screenwriting. In the beginning of each chapter,

2

you will find an expansion of the events, which answer specific questions about *Witness*.

In my writing system, we study finished films as well as screenplays. Although a screenplay is not yet a movie, its purpose is to become one, so it makes sense to look at the whole body while you're building the skeleton.

A Screenplay Isn't a Novel

Remember that, unlike a novel, a screenplay is not the final form of your creation. The goal is to have this story become a movie and be seen by an audience. Screenwriters often attempt a level of literary excellence, which is admirable but not appropriate, because a film is a collaborative medium. The common wisdom is that a film is written at least three times: once when it's written, once when it's filmed and once when it's edited. Even when a screenplay is completed, it's a work in progress.

The Key to Success

Remember that the secret of writing a first draft is:

Don't Get It Right, Get It Written.

Chapter 1

What Are The Four Magic Questions of Screenwriting?

What are The Four Magic Questions of Screenwriting?

The Four Magic Questions of Screenwriting are:

1. What is the main character's dream?

2. What is the main character's worst nightmare?

3. Who or what would they "die" for?

4. What is the resolution of the dream or a new dream?

The Four Magic Questions of Screenwriting (4MQS) are the key to effective structure through character. I call them the magic questions because they work so easily it often feels like you just waved a magic wand and said, "Abracadabra—give me the structure of my story!" And then you have it. As soon as you know how to apply the questions, you will not only get rich character development, you will be able to intuitively know your plot and begin to structure your screenplay. This is a new way of working that may go against what you believe about writing: that it's hard and requires a great deal of intellectual analysis. Working the right way allows you to connect plot with character organically. This style of creating is fun and easy.

The 4MQS allow you to organize the emotional journey of your character and the action journey of the plot. You can do this by looking at the traditional three-act structure in a new way and reorganizing it into four equal-length parts. In my writing system, it's Act II that has been reorganized as having two sections of equal length, which I describe as being Act II, Part 1 and Act II, Part 2. Once you have learned how to apply the 4MQS within this structure, you will see how this new paradigm shift will help you design a better story.

When I became a writer, I couldn't believe that doing something that was natural to me had to be so difficult and the outcome so often unsatisfactory. I studied books on writing, and the process as it was taught to me seemed flawed. My common sense rebelled at the idea that such a necessary skill had to be so difficult to master. So many of the scripts I worked on myself, or read as a teacher, had the same kinds of problems regardless of the talent level of the writer—passive heroes, poor structure, predictable plotting and flat dialogue. Also, they often took a long time to write, and for the most part were not very good. There had to be a better way.

When I compared screenwriting to building a house, the core problems stemmed from how the foundation for the screenplay was laid. So, clearly, what was needed was a better way to create the first draft. Thus The Horowitz System® and the 4MQS were born. In the same way there is a structure for pouring the concrete to form the foundation of the house, the three-act structure is the foundation for writing a screenplay. I decided to see if there was a better way to pour the concrete of the story.

What's Wrong with the Three-Act Structure?

Not a thing! The three-act structure, as defined by Aristotle, is the basis for much of how we understand storytelling—as a chunk of narrative that has a beginning, middle and an end.

Many films reflect this structure, and this structure is what screenwriters must fit their stories into. Why was this so hard? Why, if the three-act structure was perfect, were many of the writers I worked with able to come up with an Act I and/or Act III, but everyone, myself included, seemed to really struggle with Act II. This long middle section seemed to be the problem.

Why was that? To find the answer, I took classes, read every book I could find on screenwriting, reread Aristotle, asked other writers and teachers. The consensus was that this was just part of the process. But storytelling is so much a part of everything, I just couldn't accept this answer. After I became a teacher and a writing coach, I saw this problem over and over. I kept asking questions, and then one day it hit me: The answer was to ask questions. I just had to figure out which ones and what order to ask them in.

I knew that Act I answered the question "What was my main character's dream?," and that Act III explored and answered the question, "Did my main character realize his or her dream or find a new one?" but I was stumped at what to ask to understand what happened in Act II. If Act I and Act III were possible to understand, then that only left one answer to the bigger question: "Why is this so hard?" Sherlock Holmes said, "If you remove all which is impossible, then whatever remains, however improbable, must be the truth." Hard as it was to believe, I realized that it was the way we thought about Act II that was the problem.

How Could Act II Be a Problem?

How could Act II—which is an essential part of traditional dramatic structure—be so difficult to write? Act I and Act III certainly weren't easy, but they were at least possible. How was Act II different from the other two acts?

My common sense kicked in and I decided to compare it to the other two acts. For starters, it was just too long and cumbersome to handle efficiently. Maybe that was the problem. If the other parts were roughly 30 minutes/pages each and Act II was roughly double that, what happened if we split it in half?

Once I split the second act, the lightbulb came on and my writing changed forever. Obviously, it wasn't the same as splitting the atom, but for me as a writer it was pretty exciting. As I began to apply this technique, I realized there was a need for further refinement, since the two halves of Act II were different in that they each carried a different part of the story. If I could only find the right question for each section, I knew I'd be able to make the process of structuring Act II work every time.

A Revolutionary Way to Look at Act II

I explored the relationship between these act sections by watching many films and reading screenplays. I kept asking myself what the right questions were—then I had an epiphany: I understood that if in the first half of Act II the character was roughly thwarted, to such a degree that it could be described as his or her worst nightmare, it then caused the character to try even harder to achieve the goal. This added energy often sent the character in a new direction or even reversed the story told in Act I. With this added momentum, Act II, Part 2 (as I had come to call it) should have been easy to write, but it wasn't. I was determined to find a methodical way of approaching this task. I began to look at the two halves as if they were separate stories about the same characters. In *Witness*, Act II, Part 1 is about John Book recovering from a gunshot wound and trying to get back to Philadelphia to solve the crime. Act II, Part 2 is about him falling in love with Rachel Lapp. In *The Godfather*, Act II, Part 1 is about Michael Corleone deciding to join the family. Act II, Part 2 is about Michael hiding out in Sicily and falling in love with Apollonia.

What was Act II, Part 1 about then? I had always taught Act I by asking my students to identify what the hero or heroine's dream was. If Act I was about showing us the character's dreams, then Act II, Part 1 could be inferred—whatever the dream was in Act I, the next part, Act II, Part 1, had to be the main character's living nightmare.

What then was Act II, Part 2 about? After more research, I realized that Act II, Part 2 could be methodically created by looking at it as a new adventure that was generated from the events that occurred in Act II, Part 1. This section of the script had a different function: as a crucible to help the main character change into the person who had the strength to fight for the dream. For example, in *Witness*, the decision not to be with Rachel and the rejection of the nonviolent lifestyle helps John to defeat Chief Schaeffer and McFee. In *The Godfather* the death of Michael's Italian wife, Apollonia, while he's in Sicily hardens him into the man he must become to take over the family business.

Using a Model Film to Understand Your Own Screenplay's Structure

A model film is approximately 120 minutes, or two hours, long, so we have four parts that are roughly 30 minutes in length. Instead of 30-60-30 page increments, we now have four 30-minute chunks, which relate back to the answers for the 4MQS. Please note that many films are longer or shorter than our model, so you would just adjust your page count or minutes according to the total length of your script. Each one of these four equal-length sections can be understood by using the appropriate question.

ACT I	ACT II, Part 1	ACT II, Part 2	ACT III
Magic Question 1	Magic Question 2	Magic Question 3	Magic Question 4
What is the main character's dream?	What is the main character's worst nightmare?	Who or what would they "die" for?	What is the resolution of the dream or a new dream?

© 2008 Marilyn Horowitz. All Rights Reserved.

In this book we will be studying the film *Witness,* because the plot in Act II is a clear example of a beautifully written second act, not because it's the best movie ever made. There is a list of suggested films in the back of this book for further study, and breakdowns for these films are available on my website.

Witness began as a 60-minute episode of *Gunsmoke.* Note that *Witness* is in fact only 109 minutes long, but it is a perfect example of the kind of brilliant story we can all write. Act I has hints of an attraction between John and Rachel, but there's no development. When the writers expanded the script by developing the relationship between John and Rachel in Act II, Part 1, and then played it out in Act II, Part 2, the story became the right size for a screenplay. As a rule of thumb, the new adventure that must occur in Act II, Part 2, such as the love story in *Witness*, is not a linear progression of the main story but rather a series of events that force the hero or heroine to change and grow so that he or she can fight the final battle in Act III.

Brief Synopsis of *Witness* Using The 4MQS

Act I

Magic question 1: *What is your main character's dream?*

The action in the film: After the death of her husband, young Amish widow Rachel Lapp takes her son, Samuel, to visit relatives and must change trains in Philadelphia. While in a washroom at the train station, Samuel watches as two men savagely murder a third. The detective assigned to the homicide case is John Book, who informs them that the murdered man was a police officer. It isn't long before Samuel fingers Philadelphia narcotics officer James McFee as the murderer, much to John's distress.

Understanding how the first magic question relates to the action: John's dream is to be a good cop and catch the bad guys. With this question in mind, you can see how the plot is arranged to dramatize and challenge his dream. As you are structuring your first act, please keep in mind that you must dramatize through action—that is, *show* and not *tell* us—what the dream is. Try to understand how the characters help or hinder John in his attempt to live his dream. For example, Samuel helps John by identifying the killer, and McFee hinders John by being not only a murderer but also a fellow cop.

Act II, Part 1

Magic question 2: *What is the main character's worst nightmare?*

The action in the film: John soon discovers McFee's possible involvement in the theft of illegal substances. Shortly after he informs his boss, Chief Paul Schaeffer, McFee comes after John and wounds him in a shootout. Trusting no one but his partner, Elden Carter, John requests that all documents concerning the Lapps be destroyed, and he tells Carter that he will take them safely into hiding. Thinking of no place safer than their Amish town, John drives them there, but the gunshot wound proves to be too much for him and he crashes the car. Rachel begs the village elders to let John stay until he has fully recovered. John slowly heals and adjusts to Amish life, befriending Rachel's uncle, Eli, and Samuel, while making periodic trips to the general store to contact Carter by pay phone.

Understanding how the second magic question relates to the action: The second question helps you put your character into a waking nightmare. John is now completely cut off from any avenue through which he can achieve his dream. He is physically removed from the action, is wounded and is in a strange culture that despises his values, yet only appreciates the human qualities of gentleness and kindness that he has a fear of expressing. In your story, moving your character away from the main action is a good technique because it raises the stakes. Having the hero or heroine meet a new character who challenges the basic belief system of the main character is also powerful, because to doubt who you are and what you stand for definitely is a nightmare. In this film, Rachel's Uncle Eli acts as a mentor because he shows John a different way to be a man: powerful but without violence.

Act II, Part 2

Magic question 3: *Who or what would your main character "die" for?*

The action in the film: A nearly healed John spends his time repairing his car, and he manages to fix his car battery late one night, in the presence of Rachel. John convinces her to dance with him to a song on the radio, but Eli notices them and he condemns Rachel. She defends herself and leaves, while Eli hints to John that his time to go is near. Rachel is told that there are rumors concerning her and John, but she brushes them off as idle chatter. However, John and Rachel cannot ignore the escalating passion between them. Rachel offers herself, but John realizes that their lives are too different for a relationship to work, so he refuses. Meanwhile, Chief Schaeffer and McFee are working together to discover the whereabouts of the Lapps, questioning John's sister, Elaine, and his partner, Carter.

Understanding how the third magic question relates to the action: This is the new adventure I have been referring to. Still blocked from returning to Philadelphia to catch the murderer, John is physically healing. His attraction to Rachel becomes full-fledged passion and tests his resolve. He finds himself torn by an impossible dilemma. If he pursues his love for Rachel, he must give up his dream and live among the Amish. If he returns to Philadelphia to catch McFee, he will have to leave Rachel behind. Always try to get your main character into an impossible situation so that he or she will be forced to make a difficult choice. In other words, so that something has to "die." In this case, either the dream or the romance must die, because John can't have both. Since this film has a traditional ending, that is, one where the original dream is fulfilled, it is the romance that has to die.

Also, you can see how this new adventure grew out of the circumstances of Act II, Part 1. John was wounded and Rachel nursed him back to health. The physical intimacy of that situation created the opportunity for love to grow. Rachel was barely a part of Act I, and there is only the merest hint that she would become important in the story. A great way to see if you have a strong story is to consider whether one of the minor characters can become major, and/or part of a subplot (in this case, the Act I conflict between Rachel and John) could form the basis for the new adventure and give the hero or heroine a reason to "die."

Act III

Magic Question 4: *What is the resolution of the dream, or a new dream?*

The action in the film: On his last trip to the general store, John tries to reach Carter, but learns that he has been killed, supposedly, in the line of duty. He realizes that Chief Schaeffer is working with McFee, and he calls to threaten him. While in a modern part of town, the locals mock John and his friends. John can't contain his anger and starts a fight. The other Amish rebuke him, and upon returning to their village John realizes that he could never fit in. He and Rachel embrace and kiss, for the first and last time. Chief Schaeffer and McFee then discover which town the Lapps reside in, and they bring additional help to kill John. John and his enemies play a game of cat and mouse, and John kills all but Chief Schaeffer, who uses Rachel as a hostage, but then gives up when he recognizes that there is no way out. The cavalry arrives to sort out the mess, and John readies himself to return to Philadelphia. He says farewell to both Samuel and Eli, and approaches Rachel. He tries to say goodbye and fails, as there are no words that can convey what he has to say. John gets into his car and drives back to his old life.

Understanding how the fourth magic question relates to the action: The third act is where the resolution of the dream occurs. John realizes that he will never fit in to the non-violent world he has come to respect, so he reverts to his old behavior, thus giving Rachel up forever. He kills the murderer, McFee, and his henchman and brings his crooked boss to justice. Think of this as a traditional ending where all of the questions raised in Act I are answered in the affirmative. In a nontraditional ending John might have abandoned his old life for one with Rachel and then been challenged to deal with his old enemies in a nonviolent way.

When you are starting your story, I recommend that you at first see what ending is implied by the choices you have made in Act I before you get creative and start changing things around. Learn the rules—then break them. In *Witness*, John's dream, as it was presented in Act I, is fulfilled in Act III: He behaves as a good cop would and catches the bad guys.

In this chapter, we've discussed the 4MQS and applied them to the film *Witness*; the next step is to understand their inner workings.

Chapter 2

How The Four Magic Questions of Screenwriting Work

How The Four Magic Questions of Screenwriting Work

The 4MQS are part of my writing method, The Horowitz System®, which is based on more than 10 years of working with hundreds of screenwriters. The core principle of the method is that developing your characters first is a more efficient way to write a screenplay.

The first step is not to hammer out a blow-by-blow scenario, but to let the plot elements float while you figure out what your characters want. But since it's human to want to have structure, I designed the 4MQS as a way to do plot-oriented character development, and character-oriented plot development. The resolution of this seeming paradox is, ironically, not to resolve it, but rather to move from plot to character and back with ease, and without assigning either one the greater value. It's only when you gain this fluidity that you will be able to create organically, which is the goal of any successful artist in any field, writing included.

In this book, you will apply the 4MQS this way: Once you have a basic idea of the kind of story you want to tell, for example a mystery or a comedy, you'll be able to create your characters fully before you design a specific plot. The goal here is to be comfortable organizing the structure of your script by thinking in terms of the relationship between what happens and who it's happening to. Everything that occurs in a work of drama is about relationships—or should be.

Understand the Relationship Between the Questions

By understanding what the questions are and how they work together, you'll be amazed at the ease with which you can find and structure your screenplay.

The key is that the questions have a specific relationship to each other and to the story as a whole. Magic questions 1 and 2 are useful diagnostic tools because they offer a different way to analyze the traditional three-act structure by defining the relationship between the acts in the following way: Act I sets up the dream and Act III resolves it. Act II, Part 1 is the exact opposite of Act I, because the dream becomes the nightmare. Act II, Part 2 is how your main character deals with what's happened. It's also a new adventure that takes the script in a new direction and resolves the conflict by the end of the act, so Act III can resolve the original dream.

Your Hero or Heroine and Villain or Obstacle Are Always Having a Relationship

The other part of the magic comes not only from understanding your hero or heroine but also from developing your villain or obstacle, because they are the reason your main character has for being in your film. If there's nothing or no one to fight against, there's no story. Treat your obstacle or villain with the same respect as your main character. By developing the obstacle or villain, it becomes an enjoyable and relatively simple matter to structure the plot, because what the characters are fighting for is clear. For example, in *Witness*, one side wants to bring the murderer to justice and the other wants to prevent that from happening. If you can have that degree of clarity when thinking about your own screenplay, you will do a good job writing the first draft.

You Are a Character in Every Screenplay You Will Ever Write

In order to write a good screenplay, you as the writer must take big chances by making strong choices about the story you are telling. But how can we make the right choices when we are beginning a new project? The answer is simple: know your material really well. The 4MQS will help you gain a thorough overview of character and story, but you will still have to deal with the self-doubting nature of most writers. Let's now look at how we can ensure success.

There is usually one reason why screenplays don't get written: fear. The fear of being wrong is often the underlying cause, and we can conquer this fear by knowing how to respond to the feeling. If you have some good tricks to overcome this fear, your chances of writing your screenplay will improve 100 percent. The techniques and processes below address our natural fears of being wrong. Whenever you feel a hesitation or concern, ask yourself two simple questions:

1. What don't I know yet?
2. Is it a character issue or a plot issue?

Once you get an answer, you can use one of the following exercises.

Exercise 1: *The Coin Toss*

A tried and true method when you're unsure of which way to go is to flip a coin. Writers are often faced with many possibilities, and finding the right one seems overwhelming because there are just too many options. By limiting your choices to two possibilities, the chance of being right becomes 50 percent. Being willing to compress these concepts in an either/or, heads-or-tails way means you have already won half the battle. There's something about limiting the number of choices you give yourself that will lead you to clarity in plotting. The next part is to see which of these black-or-white decisions is right for your screenplay idea.

To use this exercise, you simply assign each side of the coin a choice, then flip it. For example, tails could be a happy ending, heads a sad one. Make a choice, flip the coin and whatever way it lands, follow that outcome. Try writing down what the outcome would be for your story, and if it feels wrong, simply go in the exact opposite direction. The magic in this exercise is that by making one strong choice, you will immediately know if you are right, and that if you aren't, making an opposite choice probably will be. My students are always raving about this because it's great to feel that being wrong can be almost as helpful as being right.

Take your characters with you on a typical day. The quickest way to know your characters is to compare them to yourself and the other characters by putting them into everyday situations and imagining how they would behave. It's often hard to know what your characters want, and you may have trouble structuring the right plot. While it's tricky to know what the right choice is, it's easy to know what the wrong choice is. The truth is we are all experts on what we don't want. So, when you're confronted with a plot choice, no matter how small, ask yourself what you would choose, and then what your hero and villain would choose. For example, if your script were *The Silence of the Lambs*, and you were deciding on what wine to order with a meal, you would know that Hannibal Lecter would order "a nice Chianti," and Clarice Starling would probably order beer.

Exercise 2: *Interview Your Villain and then Your Hero or Heroine*

This is a brainstorming technique that has been designed to help you get to know your characters more deeply. You will have to guess what your characters would say, and since they are your characters, you can't guess wrong. This exercise asks you to play different roles: interviewer, villain and hero. Creating an imaginary dialogue between characters is good practice for scene writing.

Set a timer for 10 minutes. Because you can't really interview yourself, first, interview your villain. Working villain first is the best way to understand your story. It's like the technique in painting where you learn to draw the space around the subject of your picture. Remember that all villains are heroes in their own minds. You are trying to find his or her dream.

The questions you will ask are:

1. Your house is on fire—you have time to save three things or people. What are they and why?
2. What food would you take to a desert island and why?
3. What other job would you have liked to have done and why?
4. What is your favorite sport and why?

Decide what kind of interviewer you will be for the exercise. For example, are you a friend, a bartender, a therapist or an anonymous interviewer? Giving yourself a role is fun and helps focus the way your characters answer by determining your relationship. In the example below, we are going to interview Chief Schaeffer, John Book's boss in *Witness*, and play both roles. These are the questions that you as the interviewer will be asking your characters. Remember the goal is to guess, take an intuitive leap and go with your gut.

Example (I choose to be an anonymous narrator):

Interviewer: Your house is on fire—you have time to save three things or people. What are they and why?

Chief Schaeffer: My gun, my wife, my child. If there was time, my dog.

Interviewer: What food would you take to a desert island and why?

Chief Schaeffer: Cheeseburgers and beer. They taste good.

Interviewer: What other job would you have liked to have done and why?

Chief Schaeffer: A pirate in the olden days. How great to be able to just take what you want without having to obey laws!

Interviewer: What is your favorite sport and why?

Chief Schaeffer: College basketball. I went to school on a scholarship, but then hurt my ankle. I left to become a cop and now I feel bitter at missing out on a richer life. I was cheated.

In my example, I have no idea if I'm right, because he's not my character. However, I do feel that I now know him better, which is the key. When you do this exercise for your characters, you will have a sense of knowing them as if they were real people. If you know your characters well, you can plot better because you have a clearer sense of what concerns them the most and how that makes them behave. The great acting teacher Constantin Stanislavski tells us that character is behavior, and this is the link I want you to make, because then the relationship between plot and character is clear: The character shapes the plot, and the plot shapes the character.

Now do the exercise for your villain or obstacle.

1. **Your house is on fire—you have time to save three things or people. What are they and why?**

2. What food would you take to a desert island and why?

3. What other job would you have liked to have done and why?

4. What is your favorite sport and why?

Now you'll want to repeat the exercise for your hero or heroine. For example, here's a sample with me as the interviewer speaking with John Book.

Interviewer: Your house is on fire—you have time to save three things or people. What are they and why?

John: My gun, my badge and my sister. They are the only things that matter to me.

Interviewer: What food would you take to a desert island and why?

John: Hot dogs, because I would think of the first meal I had with Rachel.

Interviewer: What other job would you have liked to have done and why?

John: Be a carpenter because I like to fix things and solve problems.

Interviewer: What is your favorite sport and why?

John: College basketball, because I watch it with my boss.

Now set your timer and answer the questions for your hero or heroine in the spaces provided below.

1. **Your house is on fire—you have time to save three things or people. What are they and why?**

2. **What food would you take to a desert island and why?**

3. **What other job would you have liked to have done and why?**

4. What is your favorite sport and why?

As you read, keep your own screenplay in mind and compare it with the examples given in this book. Some people are afraid of studying other writers' work for fear of copying. Well, don't worry about copying, because you are studying completed films, not screenplays, and secondly, it's actually harder than most people realize to copy great work. All great artists are inspired by others. The technique is to find a film that is in some way similar to the one you intend to write and to examine it on a scene-by-scene basis, as I will be doing with the film *Witness* later.

The more you can truly imagine your screenplay as if it were a completed movie, the more likely it will become one.

Describe a Scene from Your Screenplay Here as if You Were Writing an Essay

Begin with the time of day and the weather. Then describe the place, then your characters and what happens with them—with or without dialogue. The important thing is to see it in your mind's eye.

These exercises will help you develop your screenplay organically. Take risks and try to think of the most unlikely situations so you can continually challenge yourself into greatness.

Before you actually structure your film, it's important to understand each question separately, so please read the next four chapters before plotting your screenplay.

Chapter 3

Question 1 (Act I):

What is the Main Character's Dream?

The Four Magic Questions of Screenwriting – Breakdown of *Witness*

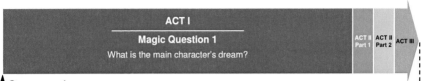

ACT I

Magic Question 1

What is the main character's dream?

ACT II Part 1 | ACT II Part 2 | ACT III

Sequence 1.

An Amish funeral is held for Rachel Lapp's husband, Jacob (3:41)

Daniel, who yearns for Rachel, consoles the grieving widow (5:30)

Samuel and Rachel go to the city, Daniel and Rachel's uncle, Eli, see them off (7:53)

Train to Baltimore is delayed, Samuel and Rachel must wait in the station (10:20)

Sequence 2.

While in the station bathroom, Samuel witnesses a murder (13:46)

McFee hears Samuel and searches stalls but does not catch him (15:44)

Detective John Book interviews Samuel about the murder (17:14)

Sequence 3.

Rachel does not want any part of the investigation (20:44)

John makes her stay the night at his sister Elaine's house (21:28)

Rachel reiterates her wish to leave (23:03)

Samuel recognizes McFee in a newspaper clipping at the police department (27:54)

Question 1 (Act I): *What is the Main Character's Dream?*

ACT I	ACT II, Part 1	ACT II, Part 2	ACT III
Magic Question 1	Magic Question 2	Magic Question 3	Magic Question 4
What is the main character's dream?	What is the main character's worst nightmare?	Who or what would they "die" for?	What is the resolution of the dream or a new dream?

What is your dream? To write and sell a screenplay, right? Maybe direct and/or finance a movie? This is a destination, a place we want to reach. We live for our dreams, and our lives are a journey to reach that destination. When we go to the movies, we want to share someone else's journey. Why do we go? We want to feel a connection to the world and other people, and it allows us to experience a kind of emotional release. This catharsis is in part what helps us decide if we have seen a good picture or not.

Every life plan begins with a dream. Your dream was to write this screenplay and sell it or direct it. Now ask yourself: What is your hero's dream?

For example, in *Witness*, John Book is an honest homicide detective in Philadelphia who must solve the murder of a fellow cop. His dream is to solve the murder.

Please complete the exercise below and be open to either confirming the dream you selected for your main character or finding a new one.

Exercise: *How to Find Your Character's Dream*

A quick way to connect to this idea is to write a first-person narration of the opening events of the screenplay as if you yourself were the main character. Understanding the way a character thinks and feels about the situation you have placed them in can cut your writing time in half, because how they feel is a clue to whether they are moving toward their dream.

Think of how the beginning of the film *Goodfellas* puts you right into the hero's dream. Henry Hill's narration opens, "To me, being a gangster was better than being the president of the United States." The camera pans out of his childhood bedroom window and holds on six well-dressed hoods hanging out at a taxi stand. The narration continues, "I knew I wanted to be part of them. It was there I belonged." You can borrow the idea of the character explaining himself or herself to the audience no matter what kind of story you are trying to tell, because you will use this technique as a tool for exploration only. Don't assume everything you write has to go into the script, though you will often get a great line or two from this exercise.

Here's the technique: Write as your hero or heroine. Find a way to physically mimic your character by finding a gesture and a sitting position that they would use. For example, in a recent seminar I taught on character development, Nate, one of my students, was having a terrible time understanding his female protagonist. He was a large man with a shaved head who sat with one ankle crossed over the opposite knee. Nate was writing a comedy about a chronically late woman trying to get to her own wedding on time. In his outline, the first act was about the heroine going through the lengthy preparation many women go through to get ready for the big event. This was the right approach, but he went through every procedure from hair washing to makeup. His questions were how to decide which events to actually portray in the script and how he could figure out what was most important to his character. We had a discussion, and he seemed unable to get the idea, so finally I suggested that he try and sit the way she might sit and to select a gesture that she would make. His heroine was a flirtatious girl with long hair.

Reluctantly, Nate changed his posture so that his legs were crossed. He dangled an imaginary shoe from his left foot and twirled his imaginary long hair with his hand. I asked the rest of the class to adopt a physical posture their main character would use, and to write about them. The room was quiet for about 10 minutes, and then I asked Nate to read what he'd written.

"My dream is to be married," he read aloud. "Right now, I am trying to get to my wedding, but first I have to do 500 things that bore me ... " He looked up with a grin. When I asked him why he was smiling, he told me that he'd suddenly understood that his character didn't care about the details, but rather about the overwhelming amount of them, and that the steps that were taking so long could be combined into a montage describing both the dream and the obstacles to realizing it. His writing exercise gave him new insight into the character, and he actually used a brief opening narration that came out of this exercise.

Assume a physical posture that your character would use. Begin writing with the phrase "My dream was ... " and write continuously about the first act for 5 to 15 minutes. Then put what you wrote away for an hour or two before you reread.

John Book might have written, "My dream was to be a good cop and live a good life free from the entanglements of emotional relationships. I worked for a man I respected and had a wonderful partner. Then one day, a fellow cop was murdered in the train station and the only witness was a little Amish boy traveling with his mother ... " And so forth. Get the idea?

Now you try it:

Chapter 4

Question 2 (Act II, Part 1):

*What is the Main Character's
Worst Nightmare?*

The Four Magic Questions of Screenwriting – Breakdown of *Witness*

ACT I	ACT II, Part 1	ACT II Part 2	ACT III
	Magic Question 2 What is the main character's worst nightmare?		

Sequence 4.

John goes to see Chief Schaeffer to tell him about McFee (29:40)

John doesn't trust people in the department and wants Samuel and Rachel moved (30:41)

McFee tries to kill John, only wounds him (31:34)

John calls his partner, Elden Carter, and tells him to get rid of all files on the Lapps (33:40)

Sequence 5.

John returns Samuel and Rachel to their Amish town (36:25)

Weakened, John crashes his car (37:08)

Rachel wants her fellow villagers to treat John's wound (39:45)

Rachel takes care of feverish John (42:00)

Chief Schaeffer and McFee try to find Rachel (44:37)

Sequence 6.

Samuel finds John's gun. Rachel disapproves (46:25)

Eli tells Samuel about guns, wars and killing (49:18)

With Eli, John visits local general store to call Carter (54:38)

Samuel shows John various things around the farm (56:50)

Eli tells John to help him milk the cows (57:51)

John meets Daniel (60:30)

Question 2 (Act ll, Part 1): *What is the Main Character's Worst Nightmare?*

ACT I	ACT II, Part 1	ACT II, Part 2	ACT III
Magic Question 1	**Magic Question 2**	Magic Question 3	Magic Question 4
What is the main character's dream?	What is the main character's worst nightmare?	Who or what would they "die" for?	What is the resolution of the dream or a new dream?

A nightmare is a frightening dream that expresses feelings of anger, helplessness, extreme anxiety, sorrow, etc. The word is often used to describe a waking event that was terrible. For example, John Book might write, "Trying to drive Samuel and Rachel home after I was shot was a nightmare."

When using the 4MQS, once you know what the main character's dream is, the trick is to simply reverse the dream and see what the opposite would be. What is his or her worst nightmare? Being poor? Being hungry? Being alone? We will do almost anything to avoid having our worst nightmares come true. What does your character fear the most? What will he or she learn from facing those demons, and how will it help them realize their dream?

In the film *Witness* John fears that he will not be able solve the murder. When he discovers his boss may be involved, an attempt is made to kill John. He then realizes that Samuel and Rachel are in danger and drives them back to their home. He can't return to solve the crime because he's been shot and is forced to stay with the Amish until he can recover.

Please note that the nightmare has several elements: His boss is a crook, John himself is shot and is unable to take on the killer. The nightmare for your hero or heroine directly relates to the dream, but should also expand beyond the simple answer (in this case, not being able to solve the murder) to include a series of events that push the story forward. Try to think of it in terms of finding three events that will be in your screenplay, using the example below:

Event #1 – When John discovers his boss may be involved, an attempt is made on John's life.

Event #2 – He then realizes that Samuel and Rachel are in danger and drives them back to their home.

Event #3 – He can't return to solve the crime because he's been shot and is forced to stay with the Amish until he can recover.

Later, when you write the screenplay, you will further explore these events and break them into scenes, but for now they will help you understand how to formulate the answer to the next question.

Please note that some screenplays invert the dream-nightmare structure. For example, in the film *Marty* the nightmare of the main character, Marty, happens in Act I when he is alone and believes he can never find love; and then in Act II, Part 1 he finds love. In *Garden State,* in Act I the main character, Andrew, is trying to stay emotionally numb, and in Act II, Part 1 he meets his love interest, Sam, and decides to try experiencing life.

Exercise: *Find your Character's Nightmare. Ask What Could Drive Your Main Character to Murder*

Act II, Part 1 often suffers from not being dramatic enough, which then makes Act II, Part 2 boring. Remember that in *Witness* John is almost killed; our goal must be to make the nightmare as bad as possible, and isn't nearly dying one of the worst things that could happen?

In this exercise you will write briefly about what situations would drive your main character and his or her obstacle to commit murder. Even if your script is about characters who kill for a living, asking yourself why they chose this as an occupation in the first place can yield useful insights that can create depth to even the most archetypal cop, killer, soldier or hit man.

We know that what would drive John to kill is his duty as a police officer, but that would not be considered murder. So even though he kills in the line of duty, we can still ask, "What would drive him to commit murder?" In this exercise, you'd pick another situation, such as John having to defend his sister, and describe the situation and his actions. This would bring you new insight and might yield a new plot twist.

We know that Chief Schaeffer has ordered a murder to protect his deceit, so there's no need to expand and ask the question unless you want to find out more about him.

Another example that may challenge your imagination is: What do you think would drive Tess McGill to kill in *Working Girl*? Tess is a character who would never consider murder, but what if she found herself having to defend herself or die?

I recently read an article that discussed a study conducted by an Evolutionary psychologist, Dr. David Buss. The results of the survey of nearly 400 different murders caused him to conclude that, "Killing is fundamentally in our nature because over the eons of human evolution murder was so surprisingly beneficial in the intense game of reproductive competition." I'd always believed that only certain people were capable of this kind of violence but if the study were true, then killing is part of everyone's nature! What were the circumstances that would trigger an act of murder from people who would not otherwise seem violent? In a separate study, Dr. Buss polled more than a hundred people about what circumstances would force them to commit homicide. The results revealed that most of the participants would kill either to defend themselves or their children. What is a situation that would drive your characters to murder? Finding the answer will lead you to a clearer understanding of what your character's worst nightmare is.

Now you try it: Write about a situation where your main character would commit murder.

Hero or heroine:

Now repeat the exercise for your villain or obstacle.

Villain or obstacle:

Chapter 5

Question 3 (Act II, Part 2):

Who or What Would They "Die" for?

The Four Magic Questions of Screenwriting – Breakdown of *Witness*

ACT I	ACT II Part 1	ACT II, Part 2 **Magic Question 3** Who or what would they "die" for?	ACT III

Sequence 7.

John fixes his car battery, is able to get the radio working (64:47)

John and Rachel dance (66:00)

Eli catches them and reprimands Rachel (67:13)

Rachel asserts herself to Eli (68:46)

Chief Schaeffer questions Carter about John's whereabouts (69:00)

Sequence 8.

John helps raise a barn. Daniel mentions him leaving in passing (71:20)

Rumors are being spread about John and Rachel (77:08)

John sees Rachel partially naked, but does not approach her (79:45)

John tells Rachel that they live in separate worlds, and one of them must cross over in order for them to be together. He decides not to (81:05)

Sequence 9.

John learns that Carter has been killed (82:40)

John calls Chief Schaeffer and threatens him (84:00)

John assaults a man who is taunting the Amish (85:56)

John and Rachel kiss–a goodbye to what could have been (90:15)

Question 3 (Act II, Part 2): *Who or What Would They "Die" for?*

ACT I	ACT II, Part 1	ACT II, Part 2	ACT III
Magic Question 1 What is the main character's dream?	**Magic Question 2** What is the main character's worst nightmare?	**Magic Question 3** Who or what would they "die" for?	**Magic Question 4** What is the resolution of the dream or a new dream?

In Act II, Part 2 the stakes must be high. We've all heard the expression "a matter of life or death." This is a hyperbole we often use to describe the seriousness of something in our lives that we are dealing with. Before you commit to the plot of Act II, Part 2, be sure that something BIG happens, something that is the equivalent of a life-or-death matter for the characters. That's why stories of war and gangsters are always popular. The stakes are very high, and we in the audience are on the edge of our seats awaiting the outcome. Thinking about what your character is willing to "die" for will train you to always think of the highest possible conflict, whether death is literal or not.

A life-or-death choice can be literal—in *Casablanca*, Victor Laszlo will be killed if he stays in Casablanca—but when writing a screenplay, you don't necessarily need the threat of actual death. A life-or-death choice can be a hyperbole, as in *Witness*, where John and Rachel fall in love. His life-or-death choice is whether to become involved with Rachel. If he does, he would have to give up his dream of finding the killer. To sacrifice true love for duty is certainly what we describe in a real-life setting as a "life or death" situation. Death here is symbolic—John must "kill" his love to achieve his dream.

The word death evokes powerful feelings in both the writer and the reader. In the world of tarot cards, the death card is usually a picture of a scary skeleton, and is often used to represent not a literal death but a change in the fortune-seeker's life. The reason these two ideas are equated is because death is often a metaphor for the loss of "what is." In other words, what we humans fear most on a primal level is change. Just because we live in a physically safer world than our ancestors did doesn't mean our primal reactions are different. Thinking of change as the death of the old situation is powerful because it will keep you looking for the birth of the new one.

What a character would die for could mean a difficult change or challenge, as in *Working Girl*, where death is not literal. It's a symbolic death. Tess must let go of her old self to realize her dream and learn to see herself differently in order to close the deal and get the guy. Please keep in mind that the genre or genre-blend in which you are writing determines the level of change. That is, what your character would die for. It could even be simply an important birthday to a high-school girl, as in *Sixteen Candles*, or an important court case to a struggling lawyer, as in *The Verdict*.

By answering the question of what your character would die for, we can determine if the stakes are high enough to bring the story to the strongest possible climax.

By understanding that there is a deeper conflict beneath the surface of your stories, you will make stronger plot and character choices. Remember, as screenwriters our job is all about creating conflict, and bringing out this conflict is a great way to do it.

Exercise: *What Are Your Main Characters' Weapons of Choice?*

This is the most difficult and critical part of your screenplay, because your hero and your villain will be called upon to go on a new adventure, and must use what they know to fight. Although they may be challenged plot-wise, it's important that you stay connected to who they are.

A powerful way to stay connected is to consider the tools they have used throughout the story so far. This will also help you determine what they would die for and help you answer magic question 3. John Book will kill to serve justice; in *The Wizard of Oz*, Dorothy Gale is willing to risk death to get home; and in *Star Wars,* Luke Skywalker would die for freedom.

John's weapon is a gun. Dorothy uses the ruby slippers. Luke has his light saber.

We can think of each character's tool as a symbol that represents the true nature of their character. This exercise asks you to imagine that you are your main character and to tell us how you acquired your weapon of choice and how you used it to achieve your dream. For example, if your character were Dorothy, you might write, "When I landed in Oz, my house accidentally killed the Wicked Witch of the East. When Glinda the Good Witch of the North gave me the ruby slippers as a reward for killing this evil person who was oppressing the Munchkins, I later used the shoes to help me go home."

Write first as your main character, then as your villain in the space below:

Hero or heroine's weapon of choice and how it was acquired:

Villain's weapon of choice and how it was acquired:

Chapter 6

Question 4 (Act III):

What is the Resolution of the Dream or a New Dream?

The Four Magic Questions of Screenwriting – Breakdown of *Witness*

ACT I	ACT II Part 1	ACT II Part 2

ACT III

Magic Question 4

What is the resolution of the dream or
a new dream?

Sequence 10.

Chief Schaeffer finds out where the Amish town is (93:00)

McFee and his partner hunt John (95:20)

John kills Fergie, McFee's co-conspirator, and takes his gun (102:00)

John shoots McFee (102:26)

Sequence 11.

Chief Schaeffer takes Rachel hostage (103:00)

John convinces Chief Schaeffer not to shoot him, disarms him (104:36)

Sequence 12.

Police arrive to wrap up investigation (105:07)

John says goodbye to Samuel (106:26)

John goes to see Rachel and he can't say goodbye to her (107:45)

John waves goodbye to Eli (108:25)

Driving out of the village, he says goodbye to Daniel (109:01)

Question 4 (Act III): *What is the Resolution of the Dream or a New Dream?*

ACT I	ACT II, Part 1	ACT II, Part 2	ACT III
Magic Question 1	**Magic Question 2**	**Magic Question 3**	**Magic Question 4**
What is the main character's dream?	What is the main character's worst nightmare?	Who or what would they "die" for?	What is the resolution of the dream or a new dream?

© 2008 Marilyn Horowitz. All Rights Reserved.

Now that you have defined your hero's dream, nightmare and whom or what they would die for, this final question can be answered. Hopefully, your main character has overcome obstacles, and learned and applied an important lesson that will help to realize his or her dream.

In *Witness*, John realizes his dream and is able to end the violence using (in part) the principles he's learned living with the Amish.

A caveat here: While the lessons our characters must learn often mirror our own experience, it doesn't mean they're necessarily true literally. They represent dramatic truths. For example, John has to learn he's capable of love and accept this part of his nature. In *The Wizard of Oz*, Dorothy realizes she's had the power to go home all along by using the ruby slippers.

By finding the core event that your character would most want to change, you can find the best ending for your screenplay. Sometimes this will be obvious, sometimes not. You will also connect more deeply to your character's dream. If your character realizes the dream he or she started with, you will have an ending like the one in *Witness*, where John must atone for his inability to catch the killer and for causing his partner's death. His dream is realized by arresting his boss and returning to his own life.

While this is a great ending, it's predictable, and another kind of ending is possible. In this new, more modern, ending, the hero or heroine learns from his or her mistakes, redefines their dream and goes in a new direction. In *Garden State*, Andrew Largeman, a 20-something actor on anti-depressants returns to his hometown for his mother's funeral, where he ends up deciding to live his life with more passion and without pills. Andrew seems to want to stay sedated in Act I, but by Act III he has discovered that what he really wants is to experience life. He has atoned for causing his mother's paralysis, and it is forgiving himself that allows him to follow a new dream.

In the film *The Wrestler*, Randy the Ram, an over-the-hill ex-wrestler, has a heart attack after a match. At the urging of his friend, an aging stripper, he tries to reconcile with his estranged daughter and gets a job as a supermarket counterman with disastrous results. He then realizes life is not worth living unless he can do what he wants, which is to wrestle. So he disentangles himself from his job, his daughter and his girlfriend, and goes to fight the last match, knowing he will die in the process.

These are both great examples of this new kind of ending I am excited about. In a traditional story, Randy would survive and win the match, get his daughter back and hook up with the stripper. In this modern ending, he uses what he learned in the film to a make an unexpected choice: He would prefer to die in the ring. In *Garden State*, Andrew finds love and follows it to a new life where he is aware, giving up his old dream of staying in his drug-induced cocoon.

The exercise below is one of my favorites. You can expect little flashes of insight while doing it. Grab them and write them down. They can be gold.

Exercise: *Change Your Character's Past, Change the Future of Your Script*

Here is an example of how, if you change your character's past, you change the future of your script. In the film *Back to the Future*, Marty McFly hates his life because he is tarred with the same brush as his loser father, George, who is still being bullied by his childhood nemesis, Biff, who is now his supervisor. Marty blames George for his own failure as a musician. Then Marty has the chance to rearrange his future by literally going back and changing the past. While in the past, in order to make sure his parents still fall in love, Marty gets his father to stand up against Biff, the school bully. When Marty returns to the present, he discovers that his father has become the successful, confident man Marty always wanted him to be. Marty is then able to realize his own dream of playing his guitar at the prom.

So a great way to challenge yourself to be more creative is by asking yourself what if your hero or heroine could go back into their past, define and then change one thing that has prevented them from achieving their dream. How would your story change? You might find an amazing twist or an unexpected ending, like the one in *Back to the Future*. Did you expect that Marty would come back to a happy family?

I'm not suggesting that you actually use this idea of going back to the past in your script. It's a game of imagination where we borrow the setup as a process to help us improve our own original idea.

Step 1. Ask yourself to think about the one major thing in your life that you would like to change because you feel it interfered with you achieving your goals in life. This could be a sports injury, a love affair or something closer to Marty's problem with his dad. If this hadn't happened, where would you be today? How would your life be better or worse, the same or different?

Step 2. Now, set a timer for 15 minutes and—writing as your main character—create a monologue about what the character would alter if he or she could go "back to the future," and what actions he or she would take. Then write about how his or her life would change as a result.

For example, if your character were Marty, you might write, "I really wanted to change my dad. So I went back to the past and found a way to change his life by getting him to fight Biff. As a result, he has become more confident and successful, and so have I." It's helpful to go into a little more depth than this example, but you get the idea.

Step 3. Using the timer again, complete the exercise for your villain or obstacle.

By imagining how your villain wants to change his or her past, you can understand how you can improve your ending.

How to do it:

The technique has two steps. First, do the exercise for yourself, and then for your villain.

Step 1. You must connect with yourself. Ask yourself what you have done in your life that you regret and wish that you could go back and fix. This can be a small or a big event. The goal is for you to feel the way your character would feel.

Yourself:

Step 2. Now imagine that you're your hero or heroine and—writing as them—tell a story about something they did wrong that they wish they could change. This will often provide a moment of sudden insight, because you may realize what is really driving your script.

Hero or heroine:

Step 3. Repeat the exercise for your villain.

Villain:

Emergency BONUS Chapter

How to Find or Refine Your Screenplay Idea

How to Find or Refine Your Screenplay Idea

This chapter will help all of you who don't yet have a story, or have realized the story you had in mind isn't as strong as you thought. You'll learn additional techniques and exercises that will help you find or refine the story of your script.

Finding a Story

The traditional methods of developing stories often work well. These include, but are not limited to, reading newspapers and books, writing down and exploring important events in your own life, using a family story or a dream. You might also adapt a book or a play, find a historical event or re-imagine a myth or legend. Keeping a journal and writing down ideas is effective as well.

Confidence Is the Key

Unless you have the confidence that you can succeed at writing a screenplay, finding or refining a story idea won't be much fun. Let me prove to you that you can tell a feature-length story, and then we can really focus on helping you to develop or refine your own specific script idea.

Using Common Experiences

Most of us share certain rites of passage: birth, death, love, marriage, kids and work. And it's our human nature to want to share our experiences with others. We write screenplays to connect with other people and communicate what we know. All stories come from what we see around us. Even the most far-out science fiction has a basis in everyday life. We respond to hearing or watching a good story by wanting to tell a good story back. All of us want to express, communicate and participate in the world around us. The way stories are told inspires us to want to respond in kind. Watching good films is what makes us want to write screenplays. We have all told someone else the story of a film we have seen.

The next exercise asks you to summarize a film you've seen, following my detailed example. I have numbered the sentences, so you can use each one as a guide for the equivalent action in the movie you've chosen. You may also want to re-watch the movie. This exercise will help you understand the basic structure of the film, how many characters it has and how many plot events you will need in your own screenplay. It will also give you some of the confidence I promised you because, if you can understand the rhythm of a film, you can understand your own story and how it has to fit into screenplay structure.

Exercise 1: *Summarize a Film*

Read my example from the film *Working Girl*, and then write a brief description of a movie you admire and/or you wish you'd written.

1. Tess McGill is a feisty secretary with big dreams of becoming a player on Wall Street.

2. After her sexist boss offers her a better job opportunity, which turns out to be him pimping her to one of his friends, she returns the favor by publicly humiliating him and is fired.

3. When she gets a new job with a kindly female boss, Katharine Parker, Tess tells Katharine a business idea she has, but Katharine shoots her down.

4. While Katharine is away on vacation, Tess accidentally discovers that Katharine has stolen her idea.

5. Tess impersonates her boss at an industry party. She meets Jack Trainer, a handsome entrepreneur, who believes in her idea and agrees to help her.

6. Tess and Jack quickly fall in love.

7. When Katharine returns, Tess must hurry to finish the deal, but Katharine blocks her and takes credit for the idea.

8. All seems lost, but at the last moment Tess proves Katharine's treachery and the CEO offers Tess a great new job—with her own secretary!

Now write out the story of a favorite film. (Hint: If you're stuck, go to the Internet Movie Database (IMDB) at www.IMDB.com and read someone else's synopsis for inspiration).

Your movie title:

_____

1.

2.

3.

4.

5.

6.

7.

8.

Good work. One of the benefits of having done this exercise is that you now know you can understand what makes a good movie plot and can start to think about what your own will be. If you have even the ghost of an idea, try writing it out and see what you actually have, and then read on. Otherwise, skip this for now.

Practicing Storytelling Gives You Confidence

Remember the old joke *How do you get to Carnegie Hall?* The answer is: *Practice, practice, practice.* Professional writers tell stories all day long, using the world around them as raw material. Ninety-nine percent of those ideas and dramas never make it onto the page, but the endless mantra of organizing experience into little movies with beginnings, middles and ends is the best way to perfect your craft. Big oak trees start as little acorns. You never know which tiny acorn could become that blockbuster, critically acclaimed indie hit or TV series.

Now, let's practice.

Exercise 2: *Create a Plot Using a True Story*

In this exercise, we're going to have the fun of taking a true story and developing it into a possible screenplay idea, and then testing it by applying The 4MQS

Step 1. Ask yourself if you've heard an interesting story lately; or, if you don't have an idea yet, substitute the plot of the movie you used in the last exercise for practice. For the sake of the exercise, let's assume you are gong to use a true story.

A True Story

One of my students, Julietta, is writing a romantic comedy based on a true story she was told by her new hairdresser, Lydia. Lydia is tall and buxom, with a helmet of black hair and blue eyes ringed with black liner. She wears black mini dresses, thigh-high boots and a silver chain with a skull ornament around her neck. When Julietta went to get her hair done, she noticed a small framed wedding photo of Lydia in a demure wedding dress standing beside a tall, handsome man who looked a lot like Benicio Del Toro in a tuxedo.

"When did you get married?" Julietta asked. Lydia laughed and said, "We very nearly didn't. Our plans got screwed up, so we had to go on the honeymoon before the wedding. We were on a cruise ship for a week. We got into such a terrible fight, I really didn't know until the day of the wedding if I would get married."

Get the Concept First

What Julietta was looking for and found was a story with a strong concept. A familiar story with an unusual and compelling twist—something that feels like the punchline of a good joke. This is the kind of mental click or a-ha you want to feel when you find the right idea. *Say Anything* is an example of a film with a great concept, because the plot reverses the usual stereotype of the woman giving up everything to be with the man. A reversal is a clever rearrangement of the typical plot elements, so the story feels new. This is your job when developing an idea for a screenplay: Make it feel fresh!

Julietta's story had a strong concept with a clear reversal: An engaged couple has to go on their honeymoon before the wedding. Please always look for a possible switch or reversal when you are mining for possible ideas.

The Details Are What Make it Feel Fresh

With this strong concept, it was time to get details, and Julietta listened carefully as Lydia discussed her new husband, Franco. He was a jazz musician who fixed computers as a day job. They'd been engaged two years before, but he'd dropped her for Suzanne, the woman he'd dated prior to Lydia, and then come crawling back a year later. Lydia refused him for several months, but finally took him back. They already had a 3-year-old son named Samson, who was a musical prodigy. So was he a chip off the old block? No, in fact the boy's father was not Franco, but was the result of Lydia's previous relationship to a man named Bobby, who was Franco's best friend now enemy, but they still played in the same band! Whew.

Put Yourself in the Story

You are always a major, if silent, character in your screenplay, because you must continually use yourself as the basis for understanding your characters. You can't possibly know how they all would react to a situation unless you know what you yourself would do. The technique is like a game: Try to imagine that you are the characters. When Julietta imagined that she was Lydia, Julietta realized that she herself would never have forgiven Franco. This insight allowed her to understand Lydia better, because she had a basis for comparison.

Now, whether you are male or female, ask yourself what you would do in Lydia's situation. Would you have forgiven Franco? If you were Franco, would you have been willing to be a stepfather to a little boy fathered by your ex–best friend, who hated you because you'd stolen his girl and his son? Remember that good dramatic writing has a high level of conflict, and one quick way to create this is to make sure that your main and secondary characters each have their own individual conflicts.

Audience Identification

A powerful script idea will instantly cause you and your audience to identify with your hero or heroine, which is key to writing a good script. If you can connect powerfully with your own characters, so will your audience.

Ask "What if?" and Make a List

Next, you have to flesh out the plot a little so that the 4MQS can be applied. To do this, ask "What if?" and list the best and the worst things that could happen. What if the cruise ship hit an iceberg as Lydia and Franco were deciding to split up, and now they were stuck on a sinking ship? Or what if they survived and ended up on a remote island? What if Bobby got hired as a musician in the cruise-ship band and made a big play to win

Lydia back? This is where you would bring your imagination to the true events and expand the possibilities beyond what actually happened to what could have happened.

The Final Test: Applying The 4MQS to Lydia's Story

ACT I	ACT II, Part 1	ACT II, Part 2	ACT III
What is the main character's **dream?**	What is the main character's worst **nightmare?**	Who or what would they "die" for?	What is the resolution of the **dream** or a new dream?

1. What is the main character's dream?

> *Lydia's dream is to be married to Franco.*

2. What is the main character's worst nightmare?

> *That she would lose Franco.*

3. Who or what would they "die" for?

> *To get Franco back.*

4. What is the resolution of the dream or a new dream?

> *Lydia and Franco get together and get married.*

Julietta knew she had a good idea because she could imagine roughly how the screenplay would play out as a finished film.

Act I would take place as Lydia and Franco were getting re-engaged and planning the wedding and honeymoon. Act II, Part 1 would take place on the cruise ship, where things would go sour but they would try to remain together. In Act II, Part 2 they would break up, maybe dabble with others, test out if the first choice was right. Act III would be about them making up and getting married.

Step 2. Decide what story you're going to develop. In the space below write down the story in a paragraph or two and go into as much detail as possible.

Step 3. Now ask "What If?" and make a list of what could happen.

1.

2.

3.

4.

Step 4. Apply the 4MQS the way we did for Lydia.

1. What is the main character's dream?

2. What is the main character's worst nightmare?

3. Who or what would they "die" for?

4. What is the resolution of the dream or a new dream?

Find Your Own Story

Congratulations! You should be feeling pretty confident right now, because by completing the exercises in this chapter you have proven to yourself that you can find a story idea and flesh it out using the 4MQS. You can't stress out anymore, because you have already done it.

A Story is a Story is a Story

I've found over the years that the way you tell a movie story is pretty much how you tell any story, so now the trick is to find something that interests you enough to write it.

Four Tips for Finding a Great Story

Here are tips about how to find the special story idea for your screenplay.

1. Become Interested in People

A sincere interest in other people's experience is the most important tool you as a screenwriter can ever develop. This is an invaluable source of material for story ideas and character development.

2. Listen

People love to talk about themselves, so if you do one thing as a result of reading this book, become a good listener. This is a skill that is underrated and rarely taught. The way to listen is to concentrate completely on what the other person is saying and to respond appropriately. Always ask if you don't understand something or didn't hear every word. No one minds repeating or explaining to someone who is really trying to understand what he or she is saying.

3. Write Things Down and Always Comment

Writers write, and the more you write, the better you will get. Remember that mastery comes from practice. Writing things down is a critical part of the process, but merely reporting events, thoughts or dialogue is not effective. Writing things down and then immediately adding your reactions to whatever you've just written *is*. First record, then interpret. Keep a pen and paper handy or use take notes on your cell phone whenever something strikes you.

4. Don't Be Lazy

Good writers study life, all day, every day. Always pay attention both to what's going on around you and also to the subtext—the unspoken feelings and thoughts that are happening below the surface.

Conclusion

Think about the kind of movies you most like to watch. The film you described in the earlier exercise is probably the type of screenplay you want to write, or at least the one you want to write first. While some writers believe they have only one screenplay in them, many of my students write several scripts. Once they become confident in their ability to master the basic craft, they find that multiple screenplay ideas suddenly appear and demand to be written. One of my students, Nick, is on script number five! He's written a horror, a comedy, a drama, and a college romance, and is now starting on a supernatural thriller! And all of them are good!

I hope that I have given you some helpful tips for finding your story. Writing is a lot like falling in love. Be patient, practice and don't fall in love with the first idea you get. Always "date" your ideas, but don't rush to "marry" them.

Good luck and happy writing. Remember, ***Don't Get It Right, Get It Written!***

Chapter 7

Putting It All Together

Putting It All Together

This section is about how to use The 4MQS to actually find the essence of your story. Below is an example of the 4MQS filled in for *Witness*.

1. What is the main character's dream?

> *John Book's dream is to be a good cop.*

2. What is the main character's worst nightmare?

> *He can't be a good cop.*

3. Who or what would they "die" for?

> *He falls in love with Rachel and has to choose whether duty or love will "live."*

4. What is the resolution of the dream or a new dream?

> *He catches the bad guys.*

In the boxes below, please write the answers to the 4MQS for your own screenplay.

1. What is the main character's dream?

2. What is the main character's worst nightmare?

3. Who or what would they "die" for?

4. What is the resolution of the dream or a new dream?

Use What You Know to Start Your Story. Don't Worry About the Rest

One thing I have learned after helping so many students write their screenplays is that if you're having trouble finding your story, some other part of your brain has the whole thing completely worked out. Finding where your mind has hidden your story is a fun way to look at the process of creating a screenplay.

Learning to remember your screenplay is like a magic trick that will help you jumpstart the project. Instead of pulling a rabbit out of a hat, you are pretending to remember something that doesn't yet exist. When developing a screenplay, "remembering" is much easier than making things up.

How to Use The 4MQS Breakdown

Now it's your turn to try to visualize your screenplay, even though you haven't written it yet. Before you can translate what you see, it's useful to understand how to write for film as opposed to writing fiction. Screenwriters have struggled for years to find the perfect way to write because while there is a correlation between fiction and film writing, there is no exact equation. The table below represents this uneasy relationship.

Screenplay Versus Fiction

A shot = A sentence

A scene = A brief paragraph with dialogue

A sequence = A chapter or section

Exercise: *Write It Now*

On the following blank breakdown, write each thought or image in the blank breakdown form beneath the magic question it pertains to. As you "remember" your script, try to describe the action and dialogue as a shots and scenes. You will probably have multiple shots and some scenes for each question. Most of this will be guesswork, but as we learned in *The Coin Toss* exercise, every time you guess you have a 50 percent chance of being right. Proceed with confidence.

The Four Magic Questions of Screenwriting –

ACT I	ACT II, Part 1
Magic Question 1	**Magic Question 2**
What is the main character's dream?	What is the main character's worst nightmare?

Sequence 1.

_____

_____

_____

_____

_____

_____

_____

Sequence 2.

_____

_____

_____

_____

_____

_____

Sequence 3.

_____

_____

_____

_____

_____

_____

Sequence 4.

_____

_____

_____

_____

_____

_____

_____

Sequence 5.

_____

_____

_____

_____

_____

_____

Sequence 6.

_____

_____

_____

_____

_____

_____

Since many films are two hours long, especially classic films, the basis for the 12 sequences is a hypothetical 120-minute film. By looking at films in 10-minute sequences, it's easier to understand them. Note that one page of screenplay in proper format equals approximately one minute of screen time. Try for between 90 and 120 pages total.

Breakdown of _____

ACT II, Part 2	ACT III
Magic Question 3	**Magic Question 4**
Who or what would they "die" for?	What is the resolution of the dream or a new dream?

Sequence 7.

_____
_____
_____
_____
_____
_____

Sequence 8.

_____
_____
_____
_____
_____

Sequence 9.

_____
_____
_____
_____
_____

Sequence 10.

_____
_____
_____
_____
_____
_____

Sequence 11.

_____
_____
_____
_____
_____

Sequence 12.

_____
_____
_____
_____
_____

Connect the Dots in Your Screenplay

Good work. Now you can connect the dots using those scenes you do know as points of knowledge and touchstones to guide you. If you know what any two scenes in your story are, you can make lists of everything that will happen in between those scenes in chronological order and then decide which events belong in the script and which ones don't. Remember that you are just beginning to and let yourself experiment and explore your story in a relaxed way. The screenplay you are trying to write is in there somewhere, perfectly complete, waiting to be told.

Whether or not you feel ready to write a screenplay based on this story is a question for you to ponder. One of the beauties of the 4MQS is that you can test out your ideas without having to commit to them because the 4MQS makes it easy to explore different concepts.

Whenever you do feel ready to write, you may want to use some kind of system to get you through the first draft. I, of course, am partial to mine, but remember that I invented mine to help me and that it may or may not be right for you. Whatever method you use to get your screenplay written, keep in mind that the goal is always to find the right way, not the long way, for you.

Remember: **Don't Get It Right, Get It Written**—then get it right!

Notes

Notes

Notes

Appendix

Suggested Films

Finally, I want to suggest that you watch many movies and break them down using the 4MQS. It's also important to read screenplays—but remember, screenplays that are available are not always reliable as reference points because they frequently do not match the finished film and/or are much changed from the version that was sold. Use the finished product as guides, not bibles. Below are some challenging examples of the 4MQS in action. Good luck and happy writing!

400 Blows, The	Match Point
Adam's Rib	Matrix, The
Adventures of Robin Hood, The	Nightmare on Elm Street, A
Aladdin	North by Northwest
Alien	Omen, The
All Quiet on the Western Front	On the Waterfront
Amadeus	Ordinary People
American Beauty	Pianist, The
Apollo 13	Poltergeist
Back to the Future	Pretty Woman
Blood Simple	Princess Bride, The
Bowling for Columbine	Psycho
Bride of Frankenstein	Ring, The
Bringing Up Baby	Saving Private Ryan
Carrie	Say Anything
Close Shave, A	Se7en
Collateral	Serenity
Conversation, The	Shane
Die Hard	Silence of the Lambs, The
Dodgeball	Singing in the Rain
Enchanted	Some Like It Hot
Evil Dead, The	Spider-Man 2
Exorcist, The	Squid and the Whale, The
Fistful of Dollars, A	Star Wars
Friday the 13th	Sullivan's Travels
Garden State	Super Size Me
Godfather, The	Thank You for Smoking
Halloween	Thelma and Louise
Hamlet	Thing, The
Harry Potter and the Order of the Phoenix	To Kill a Mockingbird
In the Line of Fire	Toy Story 2
In the Mood for Love	Unforgiven
Inconvenient Truth, An	Walk the Line
Jaws	Wedding Banquet, The
King Kong	When Harry Met Sally
Last Orders	Witness
Letters from Iwo Jima	Wizard of Oz, The
Little Miss Sunshine	Working Girl
Lord of War	You and Me and Everyone We Know

Note: Many of these films have a 4MQS breakdown similar to *Witness* available at the web site, www.MovieBreakdowns.com

Acknowledgements

To my mother and editor, Louise Horowitz. I couldn't have done any of this without you.

All my students	Michael Leleux
Abraham-Hicks	Betsy Long
Dr. Joe Adler	Donna Miller
Pierre Battiste	Christopher Moloney
Ilene Block	Rick Mowat
Arla Bowers	Adam Nadler
Jafe Campbell	Charles Salzberg
Blair Chymburjehle	Siri Sat Kaur
Kate Corcoran	Tim Shalnev
Aileen Crow	Martin Sherlock
Daniel	Robert L. Seigel
Terry Dolphin	Sada Simran
Gene Gendlin	Thomas
Jack Hayes	Maureen Vincie
David Horowitz	Fred Astaire Dance Studio
Roger Horowitz	Big Red Ram Das
Gedale Horowitz	Those Who Watch Over Me
Indike Kularatne	

Publishing Information

***The Four Magic Questions of Screenwriting: Structure
Your Screenplay Fast***

Marilyn Horowitz

60 West 71st Street #1A

New York, NY 10023

For more information about Marilyn Horowitz, visit:

www.MarilynHorowitz.com

For more information about The Four Magic Questions of

Screenwriting, visit:

www.FourMagicQuestions.com

"Essential and inspiring for screenwriters at all levels, the novice and master alike. These are the best 4 Questions since the invention of Passover."

—Michael Zam, screenwriter, playwright and former head of
New York University's SCPS Dramatic Writing division

The Four Magic Questions Of Screenwriting will end the agony that plagues screenwriters of all levels: How to structure a script.

This revolutionary technique helps writers structure, write and rewrite scripts with ease. By asking your characters these four simple questions you will be able to outline your screenplay like magic. The Four Magic Questions of Screenwriting, part of The Horowitz System® of writing taught at New York University for over 10 years, has helped hundreds of writers create their screenplays fast.

Marilyn Horowitz, an award-winning NYU professor, is also a New York-based writing coach whose students have written best-selling novels, successful feature films, short films and television series.

Visit Marilyn online at:
www.ScreenWriterMagic.com.

"Creative, Organized, Efficient and Professional. Every screenplay needs proper structure and Marilyn will make sure you have it. Characters need to be well-rounded and complex, Marilyn will challenge you to dig deeper. She's a nurturer, motivator, but most importantly, if you want to get a professional screenplay finished, Marilyn will make you do it and do it in a reasonable amount of time."

—Fay Ann Lee, writer, director and producer, Falling For Grace

ISBN: 978-0-9799089-4-1

52995

9 780979 908941

$29.

Cover Art: Smiling Otis Stu
Cover Design: The Idea Works Des

www.ScreenWriterMagic.co

06-FDX-763